D0538725

WHERE WOMEN *Create*

WHERE WOMEN *Create*

Inspiring Work Spaces of Extraordinary Women

Jo Packham

Sterling Publishing Co., Inc. New York
A Sterling/Chapelle Book

Chapelle, Ltd., Inc., P.O. Box 9252, Ogden, UT 84409

(801) 621-2777 • (801) 621-2788 Fax

e-mail: chapelle@chapelleltd.com

Web site: www.chapelleltd.com

Library of Congress Cataloging-in-Publication Data

Packham, Jo.

Where women create : inspiring work spaces of extraordinary women / Jo Packham.

p. cm.

"A Sterling/Chapelle Book."

Includes index.

ISBN 1-4027-1229-4

1. Artists' studios--United States. 2. Women artists--United States. 3. Women designers--United States. I. Title.

N8520.P33 2005

747'.02'4704042--dc22

2005012698

10 9 8 7 6 5 4 3 2 1

Published by Sterling Publishing Co., Inc.

387 Park Avenue South, New York, NY 10016

©2005 by Jo Packham

Distributed in Canada by Sterling Publishing

c/o Canadian Manda Group, 165 Dufferin Street

Toronto, Ontario, Canada M6K 3H6

Distributed in Great Britain by Chrysalis Books Group PLC,

The Chrysalis Building, Bramley Road, London W10 6SP, England

Distributed in Australia by Capricorn Link (Australia) Pty. Ltd.

P.O. Box 704, Windsor, NSW 2756, Australia

Printed and Bound in China

All Rights Reserved

Sterling ISBN 1-4027-1229-4

For information about custom editions, special sales, premium and corporate purchases, please contact Sterling Special Sales Department at 800-805-5489 or specialsales@sterlingpub.

The copy, photographs, and designs in this volume are intended for the personal use of the reader and may be reproduced for that purpose only. Any other use, especially commercial use, is forbidden under law without the written permission of the copyright holder.

Every effort has been made to ensure that all information in this book is accurate. However, due to differing conditions, tools, and individual skills, the publisher cannot be responsible for any injuries, losses, and/or other damages, which may result from the use of the information in this book.

This volume is meant to stimulate decorating ideas. If readers are unfamiliar or not proficient in a skill necessary to attempt a project, we urge that they refer to an instructional book specifically addressing the required technique.

Foreword

_F_rom the time we are small children, a dream lies hidden deep in our heart. Sometimes it is shared with our best, most trusted friends; but often it is kept hidden because the possibility of it ever happening is too unbelievable to consider. Some of us dream of becoming a prima ballerina, others of playing at Carnegie Hall or performing on Broadway. My dream was to be an artist, drawing inspiration from things such as a gorgeous sunrise or the sparkle of a waterfall.

My oldest, dearest friend is an artist. As we grew up, she created what I could only dream of. As years passed, my dreams became more vivid; but I realized that creating art was not what I was best at. Upon entering the publishing field, I discovered that I was adept at surrounding myself with gifted artists.

Over the years, these talented friends have taught me that I too am an artist, creating beautiful things in my own way. Because of these lessons, I have sought to break down the barriers that keep many women from trusting in their talents to fulfill their dreams.

That is why I have created this book. The women on these pages have made amazing things happen before, during, and after making their spaces where they now create. In each of their chapters, they have answered some of the questions about shaping a space so that it helps rather than interferes with their creative process. Because there is no single approach guaranteed to work every time or for everyone, they have offered what they know as guidelines and tips to help you in your search for creativity.

So whether you work from your kitchen table, a home studio, or a full-scale production facility, it comes down to one thing: you must make a choice to listen to and honor the creativity inside of you. I hope this book inspires you to claim some corner of the world for yourself in which you can let the beautiful possibilities in your heart and mind unfold.

FROM A WOMAN'S SOUL THROUGH A WOMAN'S EYES BY A WOMAN'S HANDS

Table of Contents

Wendy Addison

Somewhere between a collapsible top hat and a clay figure of a man holding a globe (made by a four-year-old daughter), you'll find artist Wendy Addison. She creates one-of-a-kind art pieces or vintage-style paper and glass-glitter crafts that comprise the product line that Martha Stewart once made the subject of a film segment.

Wendy's shop/studio is an old storefront in Port Costa, which she calls "a tiny secret hidden Victorian ghost town" set on the banks of the Carquinez Straits, where the Sacramento River flows into the San Francisco Bay. While she holds the occasional open house, don't look for set hours. The Theatre of Dreams might be likened to the water that constantly carries boats past her weathered door—objects rise, fall, and are carried through it by creative currents. They rest where they land or flow along, out of sight.

While many would go crazy in the midst of all this creative flotsam, Wendy finds it inspiring. "I like to work in an accumulated nest of objects and papers and

Top: Wendy sits at a private desk that is home to her sketchbooks and pens.

Bottom: An antique printing press that Wendy uses to create her ephemera.

Opposite: "I hope that if a person walked into my space, they would see my imagination revealed—the best part of me."

antiques that have a history. When I'm actively working, the place is a mess; but that type of chaos just
doesn't bother me. I love to open up a drawer or an old
cigar box and discover something wonderful that I for-
got I put there," she says. It is from this "nest" that she
finds direction for her projects.

She supports her intuitive approach with such
standbys as shelves, file boxes, and the clever use of wall
space. Cigar boxes keep small objects safe; and her
sketchbooks, where all her projects begin, are always on
a broad worktable with pens and inks. Rolls of vintage
paper are stored high atop a bookcase, (almost) out of
reach of her cats.

Wendy's advice to any who want to take their creative work to the next level is, "Pick up a thread—any
thread—of something that holds some meaning for
you. Follow it and you will find other threads that,

Left and Above: Samples of some of the ephemera Wendy creates.

Opposite: A miniature shadow theatre sits atop a rack of paper.

Wendy's Tip

To launch your imaginary voyage, carve out a private space
and time, even if it's only an hour sketching in a closet.

woven together, will give you something to hold onto." By giving herself permission to approach her studio with the same fluidity that inspires her art, Wendy has created a space that feeds and reflects her imagination.

Opposite: The strategic placement of an antique display case delineates space for a print shop area. Note the antique witch's ball hanging from the ceiling.

Above: The name of Wendy's space is an invitation to make the daytime the stage on which we act out our most beautiful and fearless flights of imagination.

Right: Antique cigar boxes hold an assortment of vintage trims from Wendy's collection, including old cigar ribbons, glass pearls, and brass hardware.

Wendy's Favorite Quote

When someone asked a famous poet to define poetry, he answered, "I don't know, but people are dying every day from the lack of it." We all need somewhere we can go to find or make for ourselves some poetry.

Left: Collections of small decorative pieces are beautiful to look at and inspiring as well. Old glass jars hold antique gelatine sequins and vintage glitter. More vintage cigar boxes store bits and pieces while they wait for Wendy's imagination to find them a home in one of her fantastical creations.

Above: Wendy sits behind the front counter of her shop/studio, The Theatre of Dreams.

Opposite: A mechanical fairy dancer is suspended until the next open house, when she will complete her shadowy dance. Wendy's penchant for optical tricks and secret surprises is a thread that runs through her work.

Susan Alexander

$\mathcal{F}$or a person working with clay, a studio isn't a luxury; it's a necessity. "The clay and dust alone make it unhealthy to do this in a living space," points out clay artist and author Susan Alexander. If a home studio isn't an option, she recommends finding a public studio, which comes with the added benefit of companionship. If an artist chooses to work in clay at home, there are a number of air-dry and oven-bake clays available. They don't work for all projects but are acceptable for kitchen-table projects and small creative endeavors.

"Work-space ambience is important," says Susan. "In my city studio, the functional pieces I produced were decorated with drawings of houses along old city streets." Now that she works in the former hayloft of a nineteenth-century dairy barn surrounded by farmland, images of chickens and country landscapes abound in her tiles and decorative objects.

Recognizing her needs has helped Susan shape a functional creative space that includes having the beauty of Wisconsin farmland around her. Aspiring clay

Top: Susan sitting at her pottery wheel surrounded by the trappings of her craft.

Bottom: The broad table and extra seating welcome participants to Susan's classes.

Opposite: Like many artists, Susan enjoys working in other media. This work space is more conducive to spinning wool sheared from the family sheep.

artists often try working in their basements, she says, where it's dark and uninspiring. "This art form is so time-intensive, you really need a space where you're willing to spend time. If a basement or garage is where you must start out, display items that inspire you where you can see them, spend time, have a cup of tea and a quiet think in a comfortable chair. Good lighting is also very important. If you do not have natural light from great big windows with an inspiring view, full spectrum bulbs offer a simple solution."

A weekly class for adults forces her to clean and organize her studio more often than she might otherwise. "Being organized saves time," she says, "but when I'm forced to choose between making art and cleaning up, I mostly pick the art."

Susan's Favorite Quote

"There's no duty we so much underrate as the duty of being happy. By being happy we sow anonymous benefit upon the world." —Robert Louis Stevenson

Top Left: Susan's fiber projects are housed in a separate space, to keep them dust free.

Bottom Left: Glazes are organized numerically, which is easier than reading the labels. Numbered test tile samples hang on the wall above the jars.

Above: Birds, flowers, and other natural elements inspire Susan's work.

Opposite: A 100-foot-long dairy barn affords ample space for a clay studio as well as a fiber workshop.

Susan's Tip

Do not have a telephone in your creative space or, better yet, have one that you may use to call out but turn the ringer off and an answering machine on, so you are not disturbed. It is sometimes difficult to regroup and get back to a project after being distracted.

Kitty Bartholomew

ﬗitty Bartholomew has tried almost every craft. Chalk it up to the intense curiosity that drives her. "I just keep my eyes open and let my curious eye lead my day," she says. Approaching the world spontaneously has led the decorator and author to some very interesting places, from guest spots on Oprah to hosting her own show on TV. Yet focusing her expansive creative energy is a challenge—one that her creative space helps her meet.

Her studio is a converted garage that looks as cozy as a cottage, with its cobbled walk and lush greenery. To organize the wide array of tools and materials that come with so many interests, Kitty makes full use of a built-in cabinet with wide, shallow drawers. Raising the ceiling added space for storing bolts of cloth, and files are tucked out of sight behind a burlap curtain.

Having a central location for supplies helps Kitty preserve the creative flow. "If I have to go five places to find what I need, I lose my train of thought," she says. Committed to helping people with limited budgets create functional spaces that also inspire, Kitty insists that anyone can create a space that fosters creative success.

Top: Kitty and her canine companion, Spot.

Bottom: This inviting walkway sets the tone for the elegant comfort found in this studio.

Opposite: To make her space even more pleasant and functional, Kitty stocks floor-to-ceiling shelves with a library of inspiring books and magazines.

"Shop at the top," she says, "then go find the bargain." If, for instance, you can't have a studio, then identify the essentials and replicate them as best you can. A door set across filing cabinets makes an inexpensive worktable, and a space for creativity can be claimed with a rug, special lighting, or paint. "Ninety-five percent of the population works on the dining-room table or wherever else there's space. Start with little changes, and it'll make a big difference."

Kitty's Favorite Quote

"It's not what you don't have, it's what you do with what you do have." —Unknown

Top Left: The former homeowner, an architect, built the drawers and cabinets that now house a myriad of supplies from yarn to spray paint to fabrics.

Bottom Left: Burlap curtains hide filing cabinets, while open shelves are perfect for keeping the boxes, tins, and other containers holding supplies in easy reach.

Above: Baskets make attractive containers for projects in progress.

Opposite: Kitty divides her space into several different areas, each with its own character and purpose.

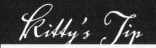

Kitty's Tip

Balance creative inspiration with a need for order by collecting only those materials that you're certain you can use. Pass on the "treasures" you don't love completely or for which you don't have an immediate need.

Anna Corba

*C*ollage artist Anna Corba's space is a two-story carriage house, the first floor of which is used for storing supplies and shipping the handmade items that comprise her product line. Upstairs, wide windows fill the studio with light and air; and when you enter, you are likely to smell an aromatic candle and hear music chosen to match the weather or time of day.

"I am complete mistress of my domain," says Anna. "I walk into my studio sometimes just to take a deep breath, and I feel anchored to my earth."

Having her own space allows Anna to be organized. "I can't think clearly amidst mayhem," she admits. With her own space, she knows that wherever she puts something, it will stay there—and that when she's in the throes of a project, she can find what she needs without disrupting her momentum.

She stores her materials neatly in clear containers and labeled drawers and baskets. While she'll tidy up during a project, she's careful not to let her desire for order interfere with the creative process. "Often the

Top: Anna and Caylus welcome visitors to the carriage house.

Bottom: The first floor of the carriage house is for shipping, a fax machine, and raw materials, allowing the upstairs to serve solely as a creative space.

Opposite: Anna's favorite worktable is typically covered with materials for a current project.

very item I need to finish a collage will be at my feet, like a sage paper scrap I discarded hours before," she says.

The key to Anna's approach to her space seems to lie in understanding what she needs in order to work fluidly. When first setting up her studio, she recognized that she would need to include empty shelves for new materials and an extra table to catch project overflow. Unpleasant distractions are forbidden, and a comfortable chair invites her to sit back and assess her progress.

Top Left: Colored furniture and cigar boxes are another way to organize tiny treasures beautifully.

Bottom Left: A cup of paintbrushes and a dish of ribbons turn storage into a still life.

Opposite Top: Broad tables provide plenty of space for works-in-progress.

Opposite Bottom Left: An antique chest of drawers with a custom paint job holds rubber stamps.

Opposite Bottom Right: Benches, baskets, and glass containers keep supplies organized and appealing.

Anna's Tip

Keep your materials organized and in view with decorative glassware. You'll be able to find what you need, and the very items that inspire your work will be visible, inspiring you to work.

Opposite: Although slanted ceilings limit shelving options, Anna makes use of the available space with low tables, benches, and a wire rack.

Above: Anna "finds" relatives at flea markets. She brings them home and color-copies them so she can use her favorites in other projects.

Right: A vintage-style cake stand holds luscious ribbons for Anna's next project.

Inspiration is important, too. Anna combines beauty and functionality, using jelly jars, sundae glasses, and stemware as see-through organizers. Bulletin boards hold poetry, color swatches, and notices for upcoming events. "My space becomes like one of my collages, layered with the interesting details that accumulate through the natural course of life."

Although Anna enjoys her studio, she's the first to say you don't need a lot of room to have a personal work space. A small table kept clear for projects, three jars for pencils, brushes, and pens, and a shelf for other materials on the side will do the trick. "The key is easy access and seeing your creative space staring you in the face, calling your name."

Anna's Favorite Quote

"The purpose of art is not a rarified, intellectual distillate—it is life, intensified, brilliant life." —Alain Arias-Misson

Top Left: Anna corrals various odds and ends in an unusual set of drawers on one of her worktables.

Bottom Left: A row of hooks makes a "visual appetizer" of items that are in limbo.

Above: Interesting glass containers can be found at antique shops, thrift stores, or your local general store.

Opposite: Wide windows bring light and air to Anna's carriage house studio.

April Cornell

For designer and artist April Cornell, inspiration is a visual thing; and the space around her helps her develop ideas. "I nail fabric to the walls and tape photos or colors along the window. As I work, the tools I use transform the place," she says.

She also starts to combine materials as she collects them. "My way of organizing is really collecting ideas and storing them in books and in piles and baskets until I'm ready to work with them. With my 'preresearch' done, I can sit down and work very quickly."

Bulletin boards are another tool April uses for visualizing design concepts. Tacks hold swatches in place, even when the board is moved, yet emerging combinations can be easily revised. Having her ideas visible helps April work. "This way it's not forgotten, the way it might be if put in a box or a drawer. When I finish a project, I fold it neatly inside a sketchbook and return the elements to their place, but only when I am done. The finished piece is so small and clean compared to the mass of materials lying around."

Top: April turns a garden into a studio with her portable drawing and painting kit.

Bottom: Plastic bins hold yarns that correspond to textile printing colors.

Opposite: April's desk in her Vermont office.

April's Tip

Gather your ideas in a notebook, a box, a desk, even a room will do. When you see them together, your ideas will start flowing.

With a boutique, an online store, and international distributors, the busy designer has work spaces in her Vermont home, at her office, and in New Delhi, India. At home, her work space started with a wooden cupboard and a single desk; now it has two more desks and a bookcase. The room is too small for guests, but at the office, she often works with other designers. "We spread out, normally on the floor. It's very cooperative and exciting and verbal. When we reach the 'to do' stage, everyone concentrates quietly on their task."

For those who aren't in a position to have one, let alone three, work spaces, April reminds us that creativity is portable. "Truly, you can transform a space very quickly. I paint on airplanes with a compact paint box and a small notebook. You can't wait for a perfect space to start creating," she says. "A stocked kit will transform a table, park, or library into a studio—and that's free."

Top Left: A showroom in Vermont displays several of April's finished designs.

Bottom Left: When April's crew works on a new collection, these rolling racks keep the styles close by in the hallway.

Opposite: This mock storefront allows April to visualize ways to present a new collection in stores.

April's Favorite Quote

"I seem to be a verb." —Buckminster Fuller

Top Left: Past projects are archived in binders covered with fabric that cues April to their contents.

Bottom Left: Another bulletin board holds fabric swatch cards.

Above: Bulletin boards make handy spaces to test out combinations of colors and patterns.

Opposite: Mannequins in the lobby of Cornell Trading's Vermont office model the current fashion line.

Cheri Ellis

*I*n Cheri Ellis's studio, saffron walls and a dark wood floor form the backdrop for partly colored photographs, spills of richly hued fabrics, and inventively painted furniture. If color were sound, you would think you had entered a jungle full of chattering tropical birds. It's a cheerful cacophony in which a red-and-orange hat is at home on a table painted with lime and black diamonds.

Cheri's clothing and millinery designs have appeared in venues as varied as art museums, craft magazines, and boutiques. "I decorate with my materials and with the things that I make," she says. Each object in the studio testifies to a period of her life, from a feather-topped chair to the nesting origami boxes that her daughter Jittania made. Cheri says having a visual history of her life fosters a sense of continuity and inspires new personal and artistic growth.

Space and philosophy merge in Cheri's home. Though the studio is usually filled with the woodsy incense, high heat, and music that keep Cheri in the mood to work, her definition of creative space includes

Top: Cheri adjusts some trim on a dress form.

Bottom: Leaving out notions in decorative containers helps prevent the over-accumulation that can occur when they are shut away in drawers.

Opposite: The air in Cheri's studio is usually filled with her preferred incense and music, and any room in the house is fair game for a project.

the whole house. "I don't like that 'you can't get this area messy' stuff. My house is just a place to shelter my daughter and me while we create."

The absence of artificial borders for the workshop helps Cheri create every day; and enhancing her space with the colors and textures that express her creativity make it easy to transition from one aspect of life to another. "It's not such a huge thing to work on a project, put it down, eat, talk to a friend. It all flows together, and your interactions with friends and family are enriched because you feel you're connected to something that really matters."

Cheri's Favorite Quote

"Live simply so that others may simply live." —Anonymous

Top Left: A chair painted with oil-based house paint led to a commission for a similar piece.

Bottom Left: The designer keeps samples from every collection, including these skirts from her Spring 2003 line.

Below: Silk brought by a friend from China led to this hat.

Top Left: Each object here represents an important moment in Cheri's life.

Top Right: Cheri often tosses around heaps of fabric when considering possible combinations for her next piece.

Bottom Left: Shelves hold files of photos and slides with samples of hats and fabrics.

Cheri's Tip

No matter how perfect your work space, give yourself permission to leave it when you need a fresh perspective on a project. Sometimes a work-in-progress needs to breathe, like a bottle of wine.

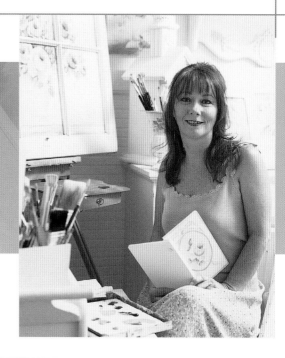

Cindy Ellis

Once, Cindy Ellis was a girl sharing a bedroom with five people; she peered into other people's yards for the roses she could touch only in her imagination. Now, the artist lives in a rose-covered world, from her own lush garden to the paintings it inspires.

Yet, as she says, "You can lose yourself to what you love." Never expecting that the romantic garden vignettes she loves to paint would bloom into a thriving business, Cindy finds she must separate art from other aspects of life. Recently, she moved her work space from a sunroom in her 1920s Craftsman home to a studio her husband built in the backyard. "Now I don't look out from my bedroom and see my work."

The new space has garden-view windows and several easels, allowing Cindy to move easily to the best light. As she works, she listens to Christian inspirational music or water splashing in the backyard fountain. She maintains her love for painting by keeping the business phone out of the studio, working in the garden, and filling a cabinet with "inspiration pieces" such as

Top: Cindy's supplies are close at hand as she sits in her sun-drenched backyard studio.

Bottom: Embellishing a chandelier with old jewelry creates an atmosphere dripping with romance.

Opposite: A settee or daybed invites an artist to rest, contemplate her work, and dream.

Cindy's Tip

Use a wheeled kitchen cart to keep supplies organized
and mobile.

rose-covered plates and Victorian postcards. "It's a happy place," she says of the new studio. "You have to have something bright around you."

Left: "There's just something about pink roses."

Above: A wooden organizer for paints hooks onto the wall, allowing Cindy to use the cart as a worktable for smaller projects.

Opposite: Fresh flowers and garden air mingle with art.

Sandra Evertson

*S*andra Evertson likes to make the most of what she has. The artist was once an antiques dealer who often found herself with boxes of such things as old crystals, wire, and doll heads that simply begged to be combined. When visitors to her antiques shop started buying the creations she calls "posh little follies" as much as for the antiques themselves, she switched to art full-time. Now she has a design company, a book titled *Fanciful Paper Projects*, another book on the way, and a world full of mixed-media collages.

Despite her success, Sandra still works from the two-bedroom apartment she shares with her husband David. She's as adept at finding space for her materials as she is at devising new uses for vintage items. The dishwasher proves a ready-made storage unit for paints, brushes, cardstock, and more; a spare shower stall holds stacked containers of feathers, beads, and other materials. The dining-room table becomes a work space with a tarp thrown over its silk tablecloth. "My husband is absolutely wonderful about it," she says. "It helps that it's just us and our two cats."

Top: Sandra prefers to work at her dining-room table.

Bottom: Cheerful paper flowers can hold place cards or notes to your friends.

Opposite: The tranquility of Sandra's home space suits her work style.

Preferring a tranquil environment, Sandra chooses silence or the old-movie channel when she works. Her mind floods continually with ideas for projects, so she stashes "emergency" sketchbooks in each room, her bag, and even the car so she always has a way to catch the creative flow.

For Sandra, a relatively confined space inspires rather than inhibits creativity. When you don't have unlimited space and budget, she says, "You have to really dig deep within. What I need more than space is imagination room. What matters, really, is the creative space inside you."

Top Left: The cabinet for this vignette, L'Opera, stands about six feet tall, including the legs.

Bottom Left: Some of Sandra's "follies" include these collage paper dolls mounted on wood.

Above: A page from a sketchbook holds the promise of the prima ballerina in L'Opera.

Opposite: With only two people in the apartment, the dishwasher is more useful as a storage bin.

Sandra's Favorite Quote

"The future belongs to those who believe in the beauty of their dreams." —Eleanor Roosevelt

Sandra's Tip

Creativity begets creativity, so keep a sketchbook in your bag, your car, and every room of the house. Not only will you always have the tools to catch and expand on your ideas, you'll find your ideas may even multiply.

Dena Fishbein

Kids, dogs, and music; you're likely to encounter any or all of the above when you enter illustrator and product designer Dena Fishbein's colorful studio. "We live here," Dena laughs, referring to three kids, three dogs, and her husband Danny. "The kids are in here from when they get home from school until they go to bed. Everyone loves to work and spend time in here. We even eat in here. It's not your regular place of business."

Located in a renovated two-car garage off the family home, the studio is the creative and business headquarters for Dena Designs, Inc., a company that provides illustrations and designs to manufacturers of stationery, wallpaper, and other products. Like the studio, the business has become a family affair, with Danny helping to run the growing company.

Combining family and work isn't good only for the mom in Dena, it benefits the artist as well, whose designs are notable for their playful charm. "There's a real creative kind of buzz in here. And I find that if you surround yourself with things that are cheerful and

Top: Dena at her worktable, which is actually two tables on casters, allowing her to reconfigure her space at a moment's notice. To avoid residues that could harm her work, the table is cleaned with a vinegar wash.

Bottom: The door to Dena's studio is always open to family and friends.

Opposite: With open shelves for supplies and a spot behind a curtain to tuck each current project, Dena keeps her workspace clear and work-in-progress safe.

Dena's Tip

Create a family-friendly workplace with easy-to-clean surfaces such as bare floors and slipcovered furniture, plenty of music, and a welcoming attitude.

happy, your work will be more cheerful and happy. You almost have to have the same mood as what you are creating."

Dena's approach to fostering a family-friendly atmosphere in her creative space seems to lie in equal doses of foresight and humor. "My space is meant to be lived in," she says, so she has machine-washable slipcovers on the window seats and an easy-to-mop wood floor instead of a carpet. Tall stools make it easy for others to belly up to a workstation to talk or join in on a project, and two tables on casters can be separated to make room for larger groups of visitors. Out-of-the-way shelves hold baskets for current projects, helping Dena keep her work spaces clear and confusion to a minimum.

These accommodations may make it more, not less, likely that she will find chocolate chips in her paintbrush container and that the kids will help themselves to her supplies; but, Dena says, "I wouldn't have it any other way."

Top Left: Dena lightens the mood in her space with "eye candy" such as this inexpensive lantern she embellished with paint and tassels.

Bottom Left: Dena recommends a flexible organizational system since, over time, artists frequently find themselves accumulating new and different supplies. Baskets and bins such as these store current materials neatly yet can be changed and relabeled easily.

Opposite: Tall stools and window seats provide ample seating, making Dena's studio a comfortable place to visit.

Dena's Favorite Quote

"The earth laughs in flowers." —Ralph Waldo Emerson

Left: The price of success for a product designer is the constant demand for storage. This cabinet, which took two days to build, features samples of just some of the products Dena has designed.

Above: Inexpensive cardboard boxes are personalized with colorful ribbons. These contain different types of paper and silk flowers.

Opposite: Neat containers and a built-in light-table grace the top of this custom-built cabinet, which also houses pull-out shelves for papers and a storage space beneath.

Andrea Grossman

*A*n avowed minimalist, paper goods designer Andrea Grossman believes in removing anything that isn't vital to a work's message when she's designing a scrapbook for friends or a sticker for Mrs. Grossman's Paper Company. "Even in my work space, I like to stick to the essentials. A studio would be nice; but because I lead a busy life and have many interests, my scrapbooking "studio" has to be mobile. I can work on my dining-room table, at the art table at the office, in a hotel room—anywhere."

Forethought helps Andrea create an art space wherever, whenever. Built-in shelves and closet organizers in the home office and a guest bedroom store albums, mementos, gifts, and craft supplies. Clear plastic containers with labels keep items safe and portable, making it easy to find what's needed and transport it to the "studio" of the moment. She also collects only those supplies that fit her personal style, such as vellum, handmade paper, textured card stock, paints, pens, and stickers.

Above: Andrea and Beau, at home.

Opposite: Andrea frequently works at her dining-room table where she can spread out her projects.

She advises artists with limited space to avoid over-stocking supplies or succumbing to the temptation to pursue every new crafting trend. "New stuff is always fun, but it's easy to get carried away. Be selective—go for the things you really love."

Left: Closet organizers allow a guest bedroom to double as a storeroom for mementos and finished albums.

Above: Built-in shelves contain a blend of decorative and useful objects, from a miniature wooden circus to cups full of pens.

Opposite: A dedicated gift giver, Andrea keeps a ready supply of presents and wrap neatly stored. A pillow featuring her Australian shepherd, Beau, adds a shot of color.

Andrea's Favorite Quote

"What things are true, what things are honest, what things are just, what things are pure, what things are lovely, what things are of good report; if there be any virtue, and if there be any praise, think on these things." –Philippians 4:8

Andrea's Tip

To keep your supplies portable and easy to store, invest in stackable containers and limit your supplies to the things you really love and need.

Dee Gruenig

*A*s an art school graduate and designer for Posh Impressions, Dee Gruenig is a perfect ambassador for rubber stamping. "If you are artistic, you can work with placement and color; and if you don't think you're artistic, you can discover a new side to yourself," she says.

Dee's home studio helps her find new ways of showing the world the jaw-dropping possibilities of this often underestimated medium by providing her with a soothing retreat from the world. White walls and a pearl gray carpet throw every hue she works with into vivid relief. White acrylic sheeting applied to the surface of second-hand furniture brings visual unity to what would otherwise be for her a distracting "hodgepodge."

Since the space doubles as a home office, Dee has a separate desk for business, which keeps the worktable free. Storing markers, paints, and other supplies over the table makes it easy to stay organized, even in the midst of a project.

Top: The toucan and fruit bowl on the back of Dee's chair was created from a stamp she designed.

Bottom: Dee creates watercolor-style compositions by creatively applying inks to her stamps.

Opposite: A scrupulously organized workstation helps Dee stay focused and productive.

The labels visible on the drawers are:

- ...mstrip, Newspaper, Banner
- ...indow Bamboo Brushstroke
- Cake, Puzzle, Tent
- ...allery Square & Backgrounds
- ...Limited—Square & Ribbons
- ...Limited—Nautical & Rustic
- ...imited—Camera, Graphic, News
- ...ted—Birthday Words & Thanks
- ...Limited Words & Invitations
- Limited Trees & Greens
- Limited—Flowers
- Limited—Flowers & Vases
- Limited—Baskets & Jars
- Limited—Critters
- Limited—Fish & Sea Life
- ...Home & Garden

- ANM Duets—Fruit & Bugs
- ANM Duets—Flowers
- ANM Duets—Party & Leaves
- ANM Duets—Seasonal
- ALTERED ART
- Limited—Duets
- ANM Flowers
- Create A Scene
- ANM—Words
- ANM—Birthday & Party Words
- ANM—Love, Cake, Easter
- ANM—Birds, Fish, Boats
- ANM—Containers, Fruit, Sports
- ANM—Leaves, Snow, Bells, Greens
- ANM—Christmas Words & Candy
- Limited—Holiday Duets & Words
- Stamp-a-Scene & Word Set

Like most artists, Dee values inspiration and especially enjoys being able to look out on an atrium that opens the small space, refreshing her imagination. In the center of the room sits an upholstered chair that is so comfortable "you completely forget your body."

Simply put, it's Dee's room through and through. She says, pleasantly, "My husband will come in looking for something and it feels like an intrusion." I say, "Let me get that for you."

Top Left: A wall unit above the desk provides flexible display space for inspiring items.

Bottom Left: Bringing the personal touch of decorative handwriting to labeled boxes helps make a work space more inviting.

Above: Dee's enormous collection of stamps is neatly organized and labeled.

Opposite: "Every time I look at this painting above my desk, I take a different path through it. There are children through the trees, on the brook, everywhere. It transports me."

Dee's Tip

Equip your space with a comfortable chair you can sink back into while you contemplate your progress. Your back will thank you for it and you just might find yourself gaining a different perspective on your work.

Charlotte Lyons

Preferring to give found and recycled objects new life in her creations, Charlotte Lyons rarely comes home from a flea market empty-handed. Everything from vintage sewing notions to game pieces to textiles, paints, and papers fills her studio. "I just have so much stuff, it's ridiculous." She achieves order with a giant cubbyhole system in her 9' x 12' studio. Built by Andy, her woodworker husband, the unit is jammed with baskets, boxes, and other containers. Lesser-used items are tucked onto the shelves behind and below the sewing table.

"It's okay to be messy at work. Creativity isn't tidy," advises Charlotte. "Make a system of organization and keep to it, even if it doesn't make sense to anyone else." For this designer, artist, and author, designing and producing projects for craft classes and how-to books demands a space that encourages playful invention with an abundance of materials for almost any type of craft. "I'm a collector—happily at work inside my own eclectic jumble of trinkets and treasures."

Top: Charlotte, creating at her kitchen table.

Bottom: A sumptuous bouquet of colored pencils begs the artist to draw.

Opposite: A large unit of cubbyholes transforms space near the ceiling into much-needed storage.

Charlotte's Favorite Quote

"Use it up, wear it out, make it do, or do without."
—Old New England Proverb

Because the former English teacher writes about projects as well as creates them, her studio is equipped for this aspect of her business as well. A computer, scanner, printer, client files, and other business-related materials are set against the wall opposite the sewing table, and a stereo keeps Charlotte's energy up with Van Morrison or other favorite CDs.

Although it's not unusual to find Charlotte working on a project at the kitchen table or knitting in the living room at night, having her own space means everything to her. "No one disturbs my process in here. I hate to put things where I can't see them; and sifting through my wall of baskets never fails to inspire some kind of creative composition—so much happens by spontaneous combustion."

Charlotte's Tip

Give yourself time to straighten up at the end of a session so you can start the next time without being too overwhelmed.

Above Left: A few glass bottles and the question, "How can I make these interesting?" led Charlotte to create this set of eye-catching vases.

Below Left: To the left of the old clock sits a collage box that Charlotte calls "Wishes" (seen open here).

Opposite Above: A windowsill doubles as a shelf for what Charlotte calls "snow globes of buttons."

Opposite Below Left: Tiny trays help keep materials for miniature paper-craft projects together.

Opposite Below Right: Named for Charlotte's grandmother, the dress form "Josephine" holds objects in transition.

Victoria MacKenzie-Childs

Above: Victoria stands before the quilt that launched her career as a home fashions designer.

Opposite: An Adirondack chair provides a perfect opportunity to have fun while using up spare paint.

For Victoria MacKenzie-Childs, artist and co-owner of Victoria & Richard Emprise, a decorative arts business, being creative "is as natural as breathing out and breathing in." In her philosophy, if you have space to exist, you have space to create; and to say you have no space "is a denial of the most natural thing in the world."

History makes a case for Victoria's argument. Though her current studio and home are in the three-deck, 180'-long Yankee Ferry, it wasn't long ago that she worked on a tiny patch of floor in a one-room apartment, sewing scraps torn from her wardrobe in an attempt to earn a little cash. "I could have reasoned my way out of just doing, being, breathing," she says, remembering this difficult time. Instead, she trusted her creative nature. "I was driven to create. I cut up my clothes and put the elements together in funny, fresh ways." Unexpectedly, a quilt she created caught the eye of a bedding manufacturer, and she stepped onto the path of becoming a large-scale designer.

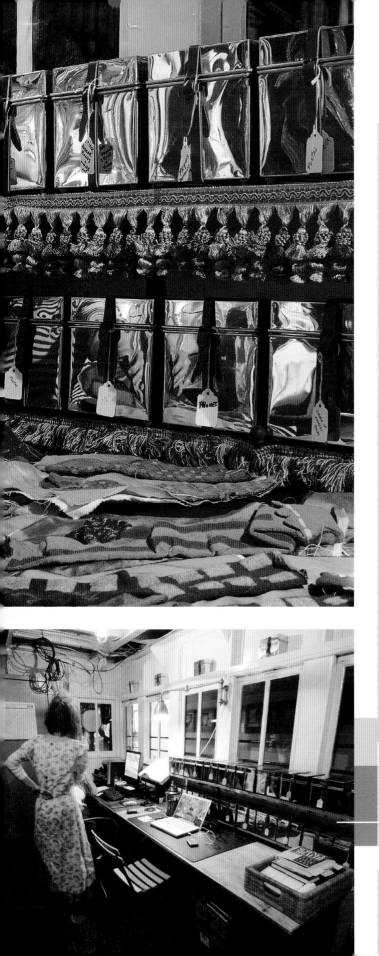

A belief in serendipity doesn't prevent Victoria from making somewhat more pragmatic arrangements. Boxes holding office supplies in her office are labeled, and to pass documents and parcels through the workshop more efficiently, she and her assistants rigged a pulley and basket system. "I love poking a joke at automation and expedition—but honestly, I thrive on order." She points out that maintaining order doesn't have to mean drudgery or spending money. With ingenuity, clean paper bags can be unique and inexpensive containers.

Though you get the distinct impression that Victoria could find something to love in almost any circumstance, living and working on a boat suits her sense of life as a creative adventure. As it rocks on the waves of the river, she designs her rugs, quilts, and other works and waits for the next shift in the creative current. "I like the creaks and the rocking and the surprise element. Where will my pencil roll next?"

Above Left: When socks for a quilt are spread across the office counter, the stainless steel boxes come alive with reflective color. There is a reflection of Victoria, pensive, in the upper-left box.

Below Left: Located in the boat's control room, the office is a focal point for managing the business. Stainless steel boxes hold tape, computer disks, and other office supplies.

Victoria's Favorite Quote

"Look, Mommy—lace." —Heather MacKenzie-Chaplet, at age 3, contemplating a spiderweb.

Victoria's Tip

Let the functionality of your space emerge from your work process and style. Keep your approach flexible so you can rearrange it to accommodate new kinds of projects.

Below: A scattering of personal treasures and a chair from Victoria's early line of furniture turn an old desk into a pretty dressing table.

Above Right: Wide windows let in plenty of light for sewing, and let Richard and Pinky peer in on Victoria and Mr. Brown's sewing project.

Below Right: With the peaceful sounds of the Hudson River and a potted garden of trees, flowers, and vegetables, it's hard to believe Yankee Ferry is in the middle of New York City.

Freddy Moran

*F*reddy Moran's love of pure unadulterated color is the first thing you notice when you enter her studio. Yellow walls make a bright backdrop for jewel-toned quilts and shelves of rich-hued fabrics. "I live in a world of color," Freddy says.

As a grandmother, Freddy feels it's important to make her space as inviting to the hand as it is to the eye. Bins of scrap fabric are fair game for little ones, and she always has time to show a child a thing or two about her art. "They start sitting on my lap at the sewing machine," she says. "Then they graduate to make their own."

Even grown-up visitors rarely resist the urge to run a hand across a work-in-progress on one of the moveable design walls or handle the fabric that is always on hand. Quilts are such tactile objects, people can't help themselves, Freddy says. "Every quilt show you go to has signs saying 'Please do not touch the quilts,' but I think that's silly. Quilts are for cuddling under."

Top: Freddy at her large cutting table. Her room also has plenty of space for fabric and four sewing machines—a quilter's dream space!

Bottom: Freddy finds that the quilts she makes in winter are even brighter: "I just crave that color."

Opposite: A cutting table does double duty with generous drawers and shelves that hold supplies, and casters make it easy to move when groups come to visit.

Freddy's Tip

Bright adjustable lighting and a floor that can be easily swept clear of pins are best for artists who work with fabric.

The home studio was built to Freddy's specifications, with a cushioned vinyl checkerboard floor that's easy on the feet during long sessions of cutting fabric and testing layouts on one of three movable design walls. A generous table has rollers to allow for easy accommodation of groups such as the quilters who meet in the studio once a week. Because Freddy loves to see color, she opted for open shelves that allow her fabrics to infuse the room with brilliance. And then, there are those yellow walls.

"Everyone told me not to paint the walls a color," Freddy says. "Kodak has identified some shade of gray that everything is supposed to look good against, but gray would just depress me. And because the hues I work in are 'pure'—no black or white added—they get along just fine with my walls."

She admits that bold yellow walls aren't for everyone, particularly those who work in pastels or muted shades. "I did once try to make a beige quilt, and I had to move into the dining room to do it," Freddy says. "But I'd never make that quilt again."

Top Left: A sewing station should include a handy pincushion, drawers for small items, a wastebasket, and a comfortable chair. Freddy has two stations set up so that a companion can join in on the creativity.

Bottom Left: A cozy reading nook invites visitors (or the artist) to take a break.

Opposite: Freddy develops her designs by pinning fabric squares to walls made of special fiber composite. A moveable wall provides extra design space, allowing her to make progress on more than one project at a time.

Top Left: Floors, shelves, countertops, and cabinets in black and white complement Freddy's riot of colorful fabrics.

Bottom Left: A closet just around the corner holds even more fabric for a prolific quilter.

Above: Small containers help Freddy keep scraps, pins, and other materials under control while she's working.

Opposite: Open shelves with fabrics stacked by color add inspiring brilliance to the room.

Freddy's Favorite Quote

"Red is a neutral." —Freddy Moran

Jo Packham

I live in an old house with so many small rooms that I can have a separate space for beading, sewing, paper crafts, or whatever is my passion of the moment. The only room in the house I never seem to get the urge to create in is the kitchen. Like my mother before me and my daughter after me, I am just not a cook.

Because my home is often used to shoot photos for my company's books, or house our artists, authors, and friends, people come in and out of here all the time. I love having all of them; but when I need to retreat, I wait until the last person leaves and then slip into my workroom. It is both rejuvenating and inspiring to have a special place where I don't have to explain myself, accommodate others, or accomplish something—where I can just lose myself sifting through a collection of vintage buttons or making something with my hands.

In my work space, there is no room for things that have no meaning or memories for me. When I look around my beading room, it is like leafing through the

Top: Jo loves to be surrounded by beautiful things that stir memories and inspire her to create.

Bottom: This antique frame was converted into a bulletin board by covering several pieces of cork with heavy brocade fabric. "It holds treasures that I want near me, not tucked away in a drawer."

Opposite: "I love the circus!" The circus-style border on the walls was created from copper-leafed Japanese papers, decoupaged onto the wall and lightly washed with a metallic gold paint.

FROM A
WOMAN'S SOUL
THROUGH A
WOMAN'S EYES
WOMAN'S HANDS

I'm So Lucky!

pages of my scrapbook. A quote Anna Corba painted over the window inspires me and the table I inherited from a treasured friend keeps her in my thoughts. The word "Hope" was added above photos of my mother after she suffered a stroke. A lampshade made from the dress I wore to my daughter's wedding creates a soft glow in the room. For me, art can turn joy and sorrow into a celebration of life and love. My space comforts me with this reassuring message.

Like many people, I think clearly by being organized. I've also found that the act of reorganizing can help me to feel clearly. Depending on what kind of week I'm having, I might arrange things by color, shape, or style; or I might scoop them all into a box and put them away for a while. Doing this clears my head and soothes my heart as much as the calming colors on the walls. I use my space to create projects, but perhaps more than anything, I use it to re-create myself.

Top Left: An antique coat rack in the entryway of my beading room displays gifts from friends.

Bottom Left: One of the advantages to owning a store like Ruby & Begonia is that I get to keep treasures like this mannequin that was made to display items for sale.

Opposite Left: Visitors are invited to take a wish from the jar on the left or one of Wendy Addison's glitter balls from the jar on the right. The hat in the middle was a gift celebrating the birth of my twin grandchildren.

Opposite Right: "Good light, a few pretty dishes of beads, and some time alone at my worktable revive my spirits."

Opposite Below: This window seat is the perfect place to decoupage favorite cards, sayings, or pieces of art.

Jo's Tip

Surround yourself with that which you love; gifts that have
been given to you from the hand and heart of a friend. It
doesn't matter that others may not understand—this is your
space and your inspiration will come from your sense of
contentment, belonging, and friendship.

*Top Left: "I have reason to believe that these are vintage
French apothecary jars, but if they aren't, they still make beautiful and practical containers for beads."*

*Bottom Left: Felt-lined drawers in a Chinese chest provide an
easy way to view a collection of buttons.*

*Above: A mini-chest of drawers makes a beautiful and practical
organizer, particularly when the drawers are the perfect size to
hold a removable plastic container.*

*Opposite: From the antique chandelier and the quote near the
ceiling to the window seat and tabletop displays, each item in
this room holds a valued memory.*

FROM A
WOMAN'S SOUL
THROUGH A
WOMAN'S EYES
BY A WOMAN'S HANDS

Eileen Paulin

Eileen Paulin knows a lot about the quest for balance. After her second child, she returned to work full time, running two magazines from a home office that simply didn't work. "I was trying to fit the space and I really needed the space to fit me," she says.

Now the owner of Red Lips 4 Courage Communications, a book production company, Eileen finds that her kids, now teenagers, need her as much as ever. "As I'm in such a time-sensitive business, working from home is the best way to stay involved with both."

To blend work and family in her home, Eileen had to design her space as creatively as one of her books. Rather than cram work activities into one too-small location, or allow them to flood through the house, she combined a room—that doubles as an office and a family gathering spot—with the adjoining garage, where a sewing station, work counter, and storage units spend the night beside her car.

Top: Eileen enjoys creating some of the projects included in the books she produces.

Bottom: "The tangible things we work with are gorgeous. If I'm ever in a bad mood, I just go out to the garage and get out the ribbons."

Opposite: Since much of Eileen's creative time is spent on the computer, she needs a comfortable chair, ergonomic keyboard shelf, and hideaway storage for files.

Stop and spend the time and money to configure your space the way you need it to be. Making the investment in your creativity can bring you—and those you care for—unexpected rewards.

The arrangement gives Eileen separate spaces for writing, sewing, and crafting, which helps her stay on top of her projects. She explains, "If all my stuff was in boxes, I'd never get out there." Still, smart use of space isn't all that it takes to make everything work. Eileen finds she must be aware of when she absolutely, positively needs to be alone. "Then I close the door. Everyone knows that when the door is closed, you don't come in."

Ultimately, what holds the arrangement together is Eileen's desire to express creativity in every facet of her life and to live as fully as she can—a philosophy that

calls for changing her space if need be. "You must have a strong base. No matter what, you're going to have a lot of balls in the air; so you might as well make sure you have what you need to make it work for you."

Left: The clever illusion of this mural is a reminder of one of Eileen's favorite pastimes, helping her maintain perspective during the workday.

Above: An antique frame filled with collectible scraps makes for an eye-catching bulletin board.

Opposite: A comfortable love seat welcomes family and friends.

Eileen's Favorite Quote

"Not merely an absence of noise, real silence begins when a reasonable being withdraws from the noise in order to find peace and order in his inner sanctuary." —Peter Manard

Left: By storing craft supplies in the garage, Eileen has space in the office to display knickknacks.

Below: A pull-down ironing board makes pressing in the garage sewing area convenient.

Opposite: Good lighting, attractive and functional storage, and a few decorative touches can transform a corner of the garage into a pleasant sewing station.

Susan Pickering Rothamel

Susan Pickering Rothamel began her art career working on the only space available—the living room floor. "I had to clean up each evening so the children could play there the next morning."

Now the multimedia artist, instructor, and founder of USArtQuest has her dream studio—1,000 square feet in the center of her home. In it, there's ample room for framing as well as painting supplies, an enamel table for messy projects, a nook for a business office, and a loft that holds a reference library and a loom. "My husband and I designed our home around this space, conferring on it the same importance as the kitchen or living space."

Cramped quarters didn't hurt Susan's ability to create, yet a more open space seems to have affected her style. "My art used to be rigid and controlled, highly organized and mostly realistic," Susan says. "Now my work is free, impressionistic, and colorful. It is as if the spacious studio gives me a sense of freedom. I can try anything without fear of failure here."

Top: Susan outside the offices of USArtQuest.

Bottom: Flat files keep art papers clean and organized.

Opposite:An enamel kitchen table provides a washable surface for working with inks and dyes.

To protect the inspirational and functional nature of her studio, Susan fights clutter from all sides. "My space may not be used as a storage or holding area," she insists. "I need it to always feel special." She also designates a spot for everything. Bulky items are stowed in a closet or large bins, and materials for certain types of activities are stored together. "Each task has its own working area," she says. "Even when my space was very small I set it up this way."

Although Susan doesn't worry about making a mess during a project, she is scrupulous about cleaning the studio thoroughly before framing or beginning something new. "There's nothing worse than getting a spot of paint on a finished work, then having to spend precious creative time repairing it."

Like many artists, she notes a connection between her space and her thoughts. "I create best when things are organized, and I believe that my artwork is fresher when I bring new materials to each project. Clearing my space helps me clear my mind."

Susan's Tip

Protect your art papers by sorting and storing them by type, color, and size. Pizza boxes make good containers for large papers and can be stored under a bed if space is an issue. Smaller papers can go into manila envelopes.

Left: A 4"-deep display box on the back of the door makes a good organizer for rubber stamps, embossing powders, and small studio cups.

Opposite: Susan balances function with beauty, with a large display shelf, a little red paint, and some favorite art pieces along the counter where she saws, drills, and hammers.

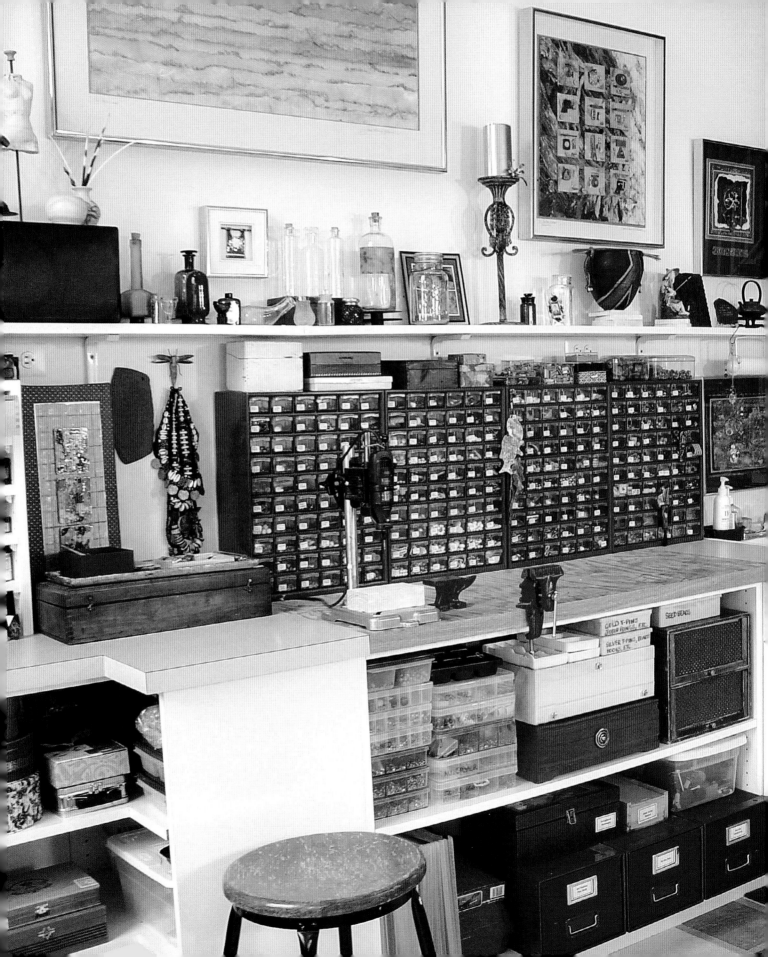

Top Left: Containers given as gifts by friends and family bring welcome reminders of loved ones into the studio, while proving useful for organizing supplies.

Bottom Left: A separate office nook helps Susan concentrate when she needs to move through business tasks efficiently.

Above: "The trick to helping a studio appear tidy is to have as many storage units as possible, all the same color."

Opposite: An island holds supplies for matting and framing, electrical outlets, and files. A generous overhang turns it into a table, and a plush rug soothes feet during a long workday.

Jill Schwartz

The warehouse that now houses Elements, Jill Schwartz's artwear and home accessories business, was 6,000 square feet of empty before Jill got to it. With a background in graphic and interior design, a solid sense of process flow, and a hard-working crew, she crafted several well-delineated spaces to accommodate nineteen employees while preserving the turn-of-the-twentieth-century feel of the building.

One key to designing a functional space, Jill says, is to think about flow and ebb. "Form follows function, as they say," she reminds us. Following the logic of how a space is used conserves energy by reducing wasted motion. For instance, Jill placed her shipper near both the office and the door, the production crew near the stock area, and the bookkeeper in a quiet spot off the front office to help them do their jobs. In her studio, labeled boxes and wheeled racks put critical materials within easy reach, allowing her to maintain creative momentum as she moves through a project.

Top: Jill and her sons crouch in the flatbed of a 1954 International pickup parked in front of the entrance to Elements.

Bottom: Visitors are welcomed by a cozy sitting area just inside the Elements entrance.

Opposite: Having materials handy helps Jill maintain the intuitive frame of mind that helps her create.

Even if your stock area is a single plastic bin and your office, studio, and production platform are a kitchen table, it's worthwhile to let how you work shape your space. Jill likes to move into different types of light as she works, so she makes projects portable by working in shallow drawers or trays. Because she works better when the height of her work surface matches the task at hand, she uses a taller table for jewelry and a shorter one for the frames and clocks from which she needs more distance.

The other key to productivity is to layer the space with the gorgeous details that make it a pleasant place to work. Vintage doors, an antique balustrade, and a bit of wainscoting camouflage modern drywall, which combined with a strategic use of paint, light fixtures, and furniture, make this industrial space downright homey. "People say they want to work here because they love this space. That's important, because we're here a lot," Jill laughs.

Jill's Tip

If you're interested in mass-producing your creations, keep items by the same manufacturer together and attach a card with the product name, style, and other information to make reordering quick and easy.

Top Left: A pretty corner is a good place to rest your eyes when working in the office.

Bottom Left and Opposite: Warm lighting and a painted plywood floor help turn emptiness into openness in the spacious front office, and an antique balustrade turns a reception desk into a statement.

Opposite: Old windows hung from the ceiling, wainscoted islands, and strategic lighting delineate space for a lunch room in the shipping area.

Above: Jill's style blends nostalgic elements with a contemporary flair, as seen in the mixture of antiques, computer equipment, and very modern curtains here in her private office.

Left: Some of the sentimental frames and scrapbooks that are part of Jill's product line.

Jill's Favorite Quote

"The barn's burnt down. Now I can see the moon."
–Masahide

Above: Old doors and windows can transform a new space with vintage flair. Here, a barn door leads to Jill's studio.

Left: Four unique antique chairs and an old Western Union sign line the wall opposite the Elements reception desk.

Opposite: Entry hall to Jill's office flanked by a pair of vintage doors. A weathered armoire houses office supply necessities while the plaster chicken family watches over all those that enter.

Debbee Thibault

$\mathscr{Y}$ou may expect an artist with Debbee Thibault's success to have a spacious stand-alone studio. After all, the company that bears her name has an entire production facility. Yet each prototype for her popular papier-mâché figurines is sculpted in her kitchen.

"It's a very peaceful place," Debbee says. "A lot goes on here, whether it's cooking, talking with friends, or creating. But when I'm cooking, there's no space at all for art."

Debbee's solution to this familiar problem isn't to make a separate space for art—it's to make a separate time. "When I work on art, I can't think about anything else," she says, so she devotes several weeks twice a year to making art. "Before and after, I focus on business and things like bills and housework."

Clever storage solutions and planning help Debbee transform kitchen into studio and back again. Paints, clay, dowels, and other supplies are organized into two

Top: A circa 1795 French dollhouse made from a steamer trunk brings history into Debbee's creative space.

Bottom: Lambee Pie, Angel of the Little Lambs, and a Dandee Cat are all Debbee's original pieces constructed from papier-mâché.

Opposite: Filled with light, the kitchen is Debbee's preferred work space.

Debbee's Favorite Quote

"What you are is God's gift to you; what you do with yourself is your gift to God." —Danish Proverb

4½'-tall plastic bins, which she rolls into the garage when she's done. Making a firm date to begin projects prevents the "out of sight, out of mind" syndrome so many of us deal with.

"This is what works for me," she says. "When it's time to start, I pull out my bins and the juices begin to flow."

Top Left: After Debbee sculpts and paints a prototype, a mold is made to form limited edition figurines.

Below Left: Debbee surrounds herself with the antique objects that inspire her work.

Above: Mr. Bunny Rabbit, A Rare Rabbit, and The Old Gray Hare are more of Debbee's original pieces constructed from papier-mâché.

Opposite: Fresh flowers, new figurines, and antiques are at home together in every nook of Debbee's home.

Debbee's Tip

Turn your living space into a part-time studio with hide-away storage containers, but be sure to commit to a time for projects.

Sara Toliver

Sara Toliver's space is less a location in which she creates than it is an outlet for expression. Walk into specialty stores *Ruby & Begonia*, *The White Fig*, or *Olive & Dahlia*, and you'll be struck by the rich variety of unusual objects and the clever displays that result from Sara's vision.

"We're located in a small town, so we tend to get local, repeat customers," Sara says. This means that it's necessary as well as fun to change the inventory and look of each store frequently. To make sure she doesn't run out of ideas, Sara collects magazine clippings and has shelves of books with inspiring ideas and pictures. She keeps them in various locations around her home and office.

While some people need a particular environment to do their best work—a table under the window, a certain kind of music—Sara finds it's all about her mood. "Sometimes I need to be in a place that is very visually stimulating, other times I need something very calming. Different things will motivate me and strike a nerve."

Top: Sara, seated in Ruby & Begonia. Her creativity shines in the decor and merchandise displays of Ruby & Begonia, The White Fig, and Olive & Dahlia.

Bottom: A special box, usually stashed on a bookshelf, keeps important files at Sara's fingertips.

Opposite: Even an office setting can be welcoming and beautiful.

Because Sara discovers and creates decorating concepts rather than objects, she finds it's not as crucial that she have a studio as it is to some. Still, moving between home, office, and the three stores is a challenge; one she handles through heavy use of a day planner and scrupulous organization. It helps, too, that work—and the books and files she keeps there—is only five minutes from home. "There isn't a day I don't have to run back and forth for something," Sara says.

There are times, however, when multiple projects and the creative process overwhelm even Sara's organization. When this happens, she makes sure she stops to regroup. "This helps me stay productive."

Sara's Favorite Quote

"What would you attempt to do if you knew you could not fail?" —Unknown

Left: Neatly ordered files and reference materials help Sara find what she needs quickly when she's brainstorming.

Opposite Top: Chic displays, like these frames and chains, make Sara's workplace inviting and inspire her creativity.

Opposite Bottom Left: Shallow drawers make ideal storage for the cards and magazine tear-outs that might come in handy later.

Opposite Bottom Right: Displaying treasured items on a bulletin board can make for a clutter-free work space.

Make your creative space a place that you are completely
comfortable and at home in.

*Top Left: A segmented wire basket organizes desk supplies
and makes them easily portable.*

*Bottom Left: Even office standards like a tape dispenser
and a stapler can bring a beautiful touch to a work space.*

*Above: Sara uses these metal boxes to store image or
catalog CDs.*

*Opposite Top: The White Fig is housed in a historic build-
ing on Ogden's Historic 25th Street in Ogden, Utah.*

*Opposite Bottom Left: The storefront of Olive & Dahlia is
located in another historic building across the street from
Ruby & Begonia and The White Fig.*

*Opposite Bottom Right: Ruby & Begonia was the first
specialty store that Sara opened.*

Sabine Vollmer von Falken

If Sabine Vollmer von Falken could, she'd put her whole studio on wheels. As a photographer, she often has to lug her gear to less-than-ideal conditions on location. Her studio, however, provides an ideal work space for creating the classic black-and-white portraits and other works for which she's known.

Wide doors open into the backyard barn where the studio's hardwood floor, track lighting, and broad space invite the imagination to expand. The work space is visually clean, allowing Sabine to customize it with backdrops hung from the rafters and props to complement her subjects. Overhead outlets free the floor of electrical cords, and wheels on the furniture facilitate easy transformation of the space.

The efficiency of the studio extends to the darkroom, office, and archives inside the house. In the office, fully stocked shelves mean she can send out a portfolio within five minutes. An arid room upstairs keeps years worth of photos and negatives safe and accessible yet out of the way.

Top: For Sabine, photography started "as a way of playing."

Bottom: Boxes labeled by year and set on shelves are an effective way to archive prints and negatives from years.

Opposite: On studio days, Sabine's commute is a mere thirty feet.

Sabine's Favorite Quote

"One day, when we have forgotten our names, the only proof that we were ever here may be those old portraits somewhere in dusty albums." —Duane Michals

"This way, I have access to everything in my space without wasting time looking for things," says Sabine. "A cleared space also offers me a sense of relief that I will have a fresh start at whatever I happen to be doing."

Top: Stocked with everything from a postal scale to a briefcase, this cabinet ensures that Sabine can quickly manage the administrative tasks of her freelance photography business.

Bottom: Sabine develops her own black-and-white photographs in her darkroom, while she sends out color film.

Opposite: Sabine periodically hosts shows in her studio.

Sabine's Tip

For anyone who uses electrical equipment, overhead outlets keep the floor clear of cables, wires, and extension cords, facilitating free movement.

Jessie Walker

$\mathcal{W}$hile photographing interiors for magazines like *Better Homes and Gardens*, Jessie Walker has had plenty of opportunity to reflect on how a room's design affects what occurs within it.

"With a home-based businesses such as mine, it's easy to end up working every second," she says. She avoids this fate with a work space that makes it easy to focus on her photography business all week, allowing her to take guilt-free personal time all weekend. She keeps out distractions such as TV, and even her collection of Depression-era glassware earns its spot in the studio by offering handy props for shoots. The office above the studio is pleasant but clear of things that could crowd the light-table or clutter the area by the computer. Wheeled racks full of color-coded files can be pulled to anyplace in the U-shaped workstation for efficient handling of administrative tasks.

Jessie's approach suggests that having a home studio doesn't mean you can't achieve distance from your work. Organization, clarity of purpose, and a certain

Top: Jessie "on location" in her dining room, where rich colors and decorative objects suit the private side of this veteran photographer.

Bottom: Jessie's photo of a Brittany-style home published in Country Living *magazine.*

Opposite: "I think about my space as an office with a very short commute," Jessie says.

measure of discipline can help you create a space in your home that puts you in a mind to work when you're working, yet free you to do other things when you're not.

Top Left: Jessie's photo of interior designer Jane Hopper's Illinois home, published in Romantic Homes.

Bottom Left: Jessie's photo of the garden and exterior of Herb Grower and Carol Franks's Wisconsin home, published in Romantic Homes.

Above: Jessie's photo of a bedroom in a Washington state home, published in Romantic Homes.

Opposite: Bulky photography equipment and trailing electrical cords make a clutter-free studio a must.

Jessie's Favorite Quote

"It would probably astound each of us beyond measure to be let into his neighbor's mind and to find how different the scenery was there from that in his own." —William James

Jessie's Tip

Save time and maintain focus on your projects by placing things close to where they will be used. Card tables make great temporary work spaces when you need to spread out.

Suze Weinberg

Suze Weinberg might not be the only artist in these pages to have a photo of Clay Aiken in her studio, but she's the only one to say so. Since her eclectic tastes also encompass Asian fine art and icons from various religions, it's no wonder that she's drawn to something called "Melt Art"—an approach to crafting that combines various media with special heat-altered compounds for a variety of applications.

As an independent product designer for a manufacturer of craft supplies, Suze is in the invigorating business of setting specifications for new materials that allow crafters to put a spin on old ideas. "Part of what keeps me creative is dreaming up new products so I can do new projects, and vice versa," she says.

To this end, her home studio is a sort of idea factory. Climb the stairs, turn right at Clay Aiken, and you're in a bright open loft lined with wire racks, wood countertops, and a dazzling array of supplies. A wood floor is both practical and pleasing in a light finish that matches the counters and wall unit. Everything in the

Top: Suze welcomes guests into her studio.

Bottom: A photo of Suze with her friends from the U.K. is at home on a shelf with projects from the future and the past.

Opposite: A kitchen counter set atop wire racks forms this island and provides additional work space.

room has its place, and she makes it her "absolute habit" to straighten up each evening. Projects from the past are tucked into cubbies with tchotchkes, reminding her where she's been and inspiring her to seek new challenges.

Though Suze usually works alone, there's plenty of room in the loft studio for guests, and she occasionally invites fellow crafters over for brainstorming sessions. "We manage to all squeeze in together," she says. "It's fabulous and it inspires me tremendously. I would love to have everyone come into my space. I even have a bed for the cats!"

Top Left: Covers of Suze's books and videos hang above a paper-craft and finishing station, reminding her of what she's done and encouraging her to continue seeking new challenges.

Bottom Left: With wire racks, supplies are visible enough to inspire, yet are organized. Clear plastic sheets lining the racks prevent the wire from indenting the rubber.

Above: Examples of different rubber-stamping techniques remind Suze of where her work has been.

Opposite: A modular wall unit organizes small tools such as brayers and bottles of glue, and displays treasured items.

exist

STAMPIN' GALS
HIA 2002
SCHMOOZE WITH SUZE!

miracles happen after a lot of hard work

FRID...

love

Suze's Tip

Be ready to show clients and students what you can do by preparing portable display boards that show off your ideas and techniques. Protect them and keep them handy in attractive hinged storage modules set in a corner of your space.

Carolyn Westbrook

"*Fabric* can hide a multitude of sin," declares home decorating professional Carolyn Westbrook designer of Carolyn Westbrook HOME home decor products. When Carolyn was a child, her mother upholstered the walls with ticking fabric and devised numerous other ways to beautify their living space. "My mother was always an inspiration," says Carolyn, now an author, stylist, designer, and businesswoman.

With so many roles, Carolyn finds her backyard studio is an absolute necessity. "I have to be able to get quiet and create. I think everyone needs a space to be creative and get inspired." If you don't have room, she urges you make it. "It doesn't have to be some elaborate space. Build some wall screens and hinge them together."

For her studio, Carolyn borrowed a page from her mother's book and stapled canvas to aged walls to cover persistent stains. She also loves to find new uses for objects, turning something like a fabric shoe holder into storage for vintage ribbons, or storybook pages into a wall mural with the help of a copy shop, a 4' x 8'

Top: Carolyn in her garden.

Bottom: Vintage candy and apothecary jars are the perfect way to display treasured buttons.

Opposite: A work space can be beautiful as well as functional.

sheet of masonite, and some imagination. To appeal to the other senses, she perfumes the air with scents like lavender and eucalyptus and chooses music to set the mood. "You have to enjoy a space where you're going to spend so much time," she says.

When her space is disorganized, Carolyn feels ungrounded and inefficient. "Then I go through a whirlwind of sorting, filing, and cleaning. Afterward, I feel like I've really accomplished something." Old-fashioned locker baskets store file folders and paint, and jars hold everything from buttons to paintbrushes.

Despite her preference for cleanliness, she also appreciates the "right" kind of clutter, such as a box of delicately colored glass bulbs or antique hat flowers. Her delight in arcane objects such as antique hangers and French bug collections has become a family joke. "I have a wonderful stuffed pheasant that I bought at a flea market," she says. "When I came walking around the corner with it, my husband and friends just burst into laughter."

Carolyn's Favorite Quote

"Success is going from failure to failure without lack of enthusiasm." –Winston Churchill

Top Left: Finding new uses for everyday items, such as sticking pens into a wire flower frog, is a playful way to organize your supplies.

Bottom Left: A wire basket keeps brushes and paints organized and portable.

Opposite: Carolyn aims to make her work space one that calms and inspires with beautiful touches such as a pot of hydrangeas and a garden statue.

Carolyn's Tip

Find ways to dress up ordinary things you need to have in your space. For instance, a little paint and an antique frame can transform an everyday bulletin board into something that's gorgeous as well as practical.

Top Left: For Carolyn, the craftsmanship that went into these wooden spools and this vintage basket make them objects of beauty.

Bottom Left: A fabric shoe rack makes an ideal holder for bits of ribbon and trim.

Above: When you love the look of your materials, your workstation can become a vignette.

Opposite: Hanging fabrics from the walls is an easy and attractive way to organize them.

Carolyn Westbrook
HOME

Nancy Wiley

When Nancy Wiley was a child, a blank sheet of paper was her creative space, open wide with possibility and invitation. Now, the dollmaker has a home studio packed with fabrics, flea-market oddities, and the other materials that go into her one-of-a-kind sculptures. In a sense, the studio itself is Nancy's invitation to embark on the process of discovery that results in her intriguing high-concept pieces.

"I get a basic idea, start sculpting a head, and take from the stuff around me," she says. "It's a little like collage." She has kept items for as many as fourteen years before finding the right project for them, but she resists putting such objects out of sight. "Having them in view keeps a dialogue in my head," she says.

The self-described accumulator prevents her materials from overwhelming the space by grouping like items in stackable baskets, placing small materials in glass jars or open tins, and using shelves for such things as a collection of miniature spinning wheels or a Red Riding Hood tea set. She organizes her fabrics by color

Top: Nancy holds "The Queen of Hearts" in front of a stained-glass window in her Victorian home.

Bottom: This tin provides a temporary home to objects in flux.

Opposite: Nancy's dolls range in size from the 28" Fairy Godmother to an 8" clown.

Nancy's Tip

Hang on to the things you find truly compelling, and wait for the right opportunity to use them. Keep your collection under control, however, by periodically culling out objects that no longer appeal to you.

and uses tackle boxes for tiny objects such as beads. A broad worktable in the center of the room and a comfortable wheeled chair provide a focal point for each day's activity.

"I don't clean up every day," she says. "I'm perfectly happy to sit in the middle of what other people would consider chaos and get my work done." She keeps it from getting out of hand with a weekly straightening. "It never seems to last long, though."

Although she appreciates clean, clear, minimalistic spaces, she can't work in one. "If I was in a white room, I'd probably fill it up. I need to have that visual noise around to be inspired."

For artists unable to have an entire studio to themselves, Nancy recommends carving out a space anywhere. "I have a friend who paints in her living room. Her family has adapted and it's not a big deal." The key to being creative, she says, is silence. "Turn off the radio, don't answer the phone. Spend some time each day just being quiet and the ideas will come."

Top Left: This "Alice in Wonderland" sits atop a lazy susan, allowing the viewer to alternate between a 22" and a 12" version of the doll.

Bottom Left: The numerous tiny objects that comprise this doll's skirt came from a collection stored in glass containers.

Top Left: Almost any object on Nancy's shelves may become part of her next creation.

Top Right: "I try to keep like things together in baskets and on shelves." Here, a basket contains a pool of lace.

Bottom Left: "You can never have too many shelves."

Nancy's Favorite Quote

"Go confidently in the direction of your dreams. Live the life you've imagined. As you simplify your life, the laws of the universe will be simpler." —Henry David Thoreau

Martha Young

Having earned a BA and an MVA, Martha Young is professionally experienced as an art educator, illustrator, fabricator of mythological soft-sculpture figures and storytelling. In 1998, she and her husband Jock McQuilkin cofounded Whimble Designs, Inc., in midtown Atlanta, Georgia. There, she manifested a fantasy creation called The Enchanted Place to protect and foster her fairy beings, the Whimbles. These beings and their companions traveled to their new home at the behest of their king, Thaddeus, who is concerned that the light is dimming on Earth much as it did millennia ago in his far away Land of Caelumen. Here to teach values and traditions that may have been forgotten, the Whimbles also encourage one to hold fast to a dream.

These tiny visitors act as Martha's muse. Their inspirations, reflected in every inch of Whimble Designs' experiential retail gallery, the artist's studio workshop, and her residence, are housed under one roof. Their spirits have guided Martha to create exquisitely elegant products with their magical sewing skills. They have also encouraged her

to design a space that is not only expertly organized but aesthetically peaceful and beautiful as well. Only in that way, can both she and they best initiate and complete any creative project.

The Guidance of Manning the Woodland Whimble

When Manning and his family left their land, they had been living cozily in a fine large maple tree, high above the floor. So now, the Woodland Whimble finds himself most content when perched high on the sliding Putnam ladder that Martha pushes from one maple cabinet to another. From here, he can breath in the scent of his favorite wood as well as feel its lustrous smoothness. As a cabinet door is opened, he peeks in to admire the neatly stacked retail products that have been completed. Since he has a fine memory, he often puts special artwork away for Martha.

Above Top: Martha and Pippin.

Opposite: Manning the Woodland Whimble is perched on a Putnam ladder that glides easily over its brass rod to reach every maple cabinet.

Surveying the room, he admires its spatial design. "Of course," he whispers to himself, "I helped her solve some important organizational problems and the results simply add to the beauty of the place, if I do say so myself."

Due, in part, to his uniquely high vantage point, Manning has always been known for his organizational talent throughout Caelumen. He and Martha had a long discussion about storage space. It is a continual challenge for her. Firstly, to enable her to place items away from view above the flat files, he suggested that she build a portable wooden frame shaped like a fire screen. He happily stitched the pastel hand-dyed multicolored China silk and added grommets to both top and bottom. Shortly afterward, he and his heart mate, Sophie, pulled ribbon through the eyelets and tied them to both the top and bottom wooden dowels attached to the frame. After finishing, they lighted the niche behind to illuminate the fabric. Secondly, the two Whimbles picked some pale peach velvet fabric to cover the space between the countertops and the floor. Martha mounted dowels to the counters and the floor. To both top and bottom of the cut fabric, Manning sewed channels into which he gathered the fabric onto the dowels. Now Martha can remove any dowel to reach stored materials.

The light colors and silky texture of the two fabrics used to create more storage area complement the smooth warm glow of the surrounding maple. Manning likes this effect very much; but more importantly, he likes the storage safely organized behind cabinets, drawers, and fabric-covered areas. He and Martha both agree that the space is rich-looking yet uncluttered and calm.

The Guidance of Stafford the Tiny Tree Frog

Stafford is the Woodland Whimbles' Companion. One of his favorite places is within Martha's ribbon and tassel cabinet. The wee frog misses the woodlands of Caelumen and the maple tree he called home, so the burl maple cabinet feels familiar. Stafford loves playing "hide and go seek" with his other friends. With his bright coloring he can easily camouflage himself on top of one of the more brilliantly hand-dyed silk ribbons at any time.

Like Manning, Stafford often hops onto the topmost shelf in the cabinet to survey everything beneath him. This is easy because the shelving is clear plexiglas. Although he had never seen this material before coming to The

Enchanted Place, he likes it very much for it reminds him of looking though one of the small still crystalline woodland pools in his land. When the cabinet was completed and shelving was being discussed, he suggested to Martha that she use the clear polished material to organize and display the ribbon. He was delighted when she did so.

Now, the cabinet is perfect. When the doors are closed, one sees only the maple burl veneer and the antique metallic thread spools, chosen carefully by the tiny frog. The effect is unusual and texturally interesting. When doors are open, Stafford makes certain that his cabinet stays organized. He dusts the shelves, stacks the ribbons neatly, and arranges the tassels carefully. All in all, he creates a most wonderful display.

The Guidance of Delaney the Pillow Whimble

One day Delaney the Pillow Whimble, stood quietly in the center of the long tall hallway of The Enchanted Place. Hearing footsteps, the tiny one scooted quickly to the side. When he saw that it was Martha opening the nearby gate, he ran up to her, pulling on her skirt to get her attention. "I've an idea, if you'd like to hear it!" he exclaimed.

Martha looked down fondly, picked Delaney up, and placed him on her shoulder. "But of course, Delaney," she replied.

"Hum. Then, you must know that I have been remembering what we did in our Caelumen tunnel homes to store our fine linens. We built tall wooden frames—that is, large by our standards. We notched the vertical sides of each frame to hold many young but strong sapling limbs. Finally, after our fabrics were washed and ironed, we hung them carefully over each of the poles. It's always been functional for us, you know, using the tunnel walls like that. But it's also very pretty to see all one's clean linens displayed so well. I think you could do something similar along this hallway?"

Opposite: Stafford the Tiny Tree Frog thinks the lines of this vertical utilitarian cabinet are handsome with doors open or closed.

Above: Delaney the Pillow Whimble admires the effect of layering organdy embroidered draperies over other fine fabrics to create enchantment in a long hallway.

"What a clever idea you have!" said Martha, already thinking about how she could translate this Whimble Colony construct into her environment. She realized that she could build a 1'-wide pine frame to fit the wall, sawing 4"-deep by 1½"-wide downward-slanted notches every 5" in the two vertical sides of the frame. The wide frame could then hold several standard wooden drapery rods with finials to keep the dowels in place. After all of the raw wood was stained a golden wood hue of her choice, she and the Whimbles would hang her best lace linens and antique children's clothing on the rods.

Although this project was completed a long time ago, the Whimbles never tire of seeing the results. Some days Delaney and Martha delight in tying back the organdy draperies to unveil this special display. Other days, they let the material fall unfettered, to create an enchanting layered effect of the gossamer fabric over lace and linen.

The Guidance of Daphne the Hillside Whimble

Daphne the Hillside Whimble has journeyed from the upper reaches of Caelumen where the light is pure and bright and plants are lush during spring and summer months. She frequently walked alone on her favorite tiny meadow paths or along the meandering clear streams of her land, carrying a carved rose quartz heart staff to guide her. At The Enchanted Place she is fondest of the room where Martha illustrates.

Sun streaming through round windows is filtered by sandblasted patterns and refracted by round, colored, faceted glass jewels that create a magical circle of light. The jewels remind Daphne not only of her own rose quartz heart staff but other gems in her land as well. Some time ago, she suggested that the studio walls be painted to look like some of the crystal tunnels that ran beneath the ground near her mountain home. With permission, she painted a small bit of plaster in the room to show Martha how she remembered these. Soon, Daphne and her other Caelumen friends had painted every inch of wall space in the small room. The texture from layering light color over dark was perfect.

Martha is pleased with the juxtaposition of organic materials and other varied elements that creates a peaceful balance in this space. The arrival of Daphne holding her

The Guidance of Sasha and Rudi the Orchid Whimble Twins

Like all Whimbles, Sasha and her twin brother Rudi have a deep appreciation and affection for greenery and fragrant blooms. In Caelumen, their favorite place to sleep was inside lady slipper orchids. They would often string hand-fashioned tiny hearts from slender leafy branches and vines. When they arrived at The Enchanted Place, they were overjoyed to see plants everywhere, even orchids nestled in among the ferns. Like their friend Daphne, they love to tend to any plant needing attention. Their wee ladders can often be seen here and there resting within a group of plants where they have been working.

Finding storage space for Martha's drawings was a problem that the Whimble twins solved soon after arriving in their new home. They located a fine set of wooden flat files and suggested that it be placed under another round window in Martha's studio. With this completed, Rudi helped to move several plants onto its surface where they grow particularly well in the bright afternoon light. Soon the Whimbles had filled each drawer with matted drawings. Now, when Martha needs certain artwork, she can count on them to find it quickly and to display it for her on top of her wooden files amongst the verdant plants. There, all Whimbles admire her colored pencil drawings and polaroid transfers of characters from their land as well as her cheerful three-dimensional figures.

heart staff complements this balance with a warmth of companionship. Although they chat often, Daphne becomes as absorbed in the drawings as Martha. Quiet reigns in this sequestered room, protected from the hustle and bustle of constant activity in parking lots and streets just beyond its walls.

Above: Sasha and Rudi, the Orchid Whimble Twins, use verdant plants and fragrant blooms to enhance the beauty of any room.

Opposite: Daphne the Hillside Whimble likes the juxtaposition of the organic world with architectural elements and studio accessories that creates a peaceful balance.

In the Words of the Caelumen King, Thaddeus

"Martha has provided a safe haven for all Caelumen visitors at The Enchanted Place. They, in turn, have given her the guidance, inspiration, and companionship to enrich her working environment. The artist and all the magical beings from my land have organized every inch of studio space with the option that any of these areas may be maintained in full view or closed with cabinet door or fabric. The result is crisp and uncluttered. In addition, the Whimbles and Martha have integrated interesting architectural elements and accessories with the organic world, resulting in a unity both calming and energetically grounding. The ordered beauty of this space where attention has been given to every detail enables Martha to focus well and to create at her best."

Martha's Favorite Quote

"Place all your dreams into your heart for safekeeping and believe that one day each will come true." —The Anciennan cat Thanu, from *The Legend of the Land of Caelumen*.

Above: The Caelumen King, Thaddeus, a three-dimensional soft-sculpture figure.

Above Right: "The Warmth of Friendship", a book illustration of the Anciennan cat Tobias and the Whimbles for The Legend of the Land of Caelumen. *(Medium: colored pencil.)*

Right: Nibbob the Terrestrial Frog, a three-dimensional mythological soft-sculpture figure.

Credits

Book Editor: Lecia Monsen

Writer: Jennifer Gibbs for McKinnon Mulherin

Copy Editor: Marilyn Goff

Photo Stylists: Rebecca Ittner, Jo Packham

Book Designer: Matt Shay for Shay Design & Illustration

Photographers:

Steve Aja Photography pages 8–15, 24–31, 50–59

Taffnie Bogart pages 16–19

Kelli Coggins page 142 (Nibbob)

B. Evan Davis page 136

Ryne Hazen for Hazen Photography pages 72–77

Ryne Hazen and Zac Williams for Chapelle, Ltd. pages 78–83, 108–113

Jenifer Jordan pages 126–131

Chris Little pages 137–141

Thomas McConnell pages 46–49

Brian Morris for Morningstar Photography pages 38–41

Brian Oglesbee pages 64–71, 122–125, 132–135

Karen Pike Photography pages 32–37

Mark Tanner Photography pages 20–23, 42–45, 60–63, 84–89, 104–107

Sabine Vollmer von Falken pages 96–103, 114–117

Jesse Walker pages 118–121

Metric Conversion Charts

inches to millimeters and centimeters

inches	mm	cm	inches	cm	inches	cm
⅛	3	0.3	9	22.9	30	76.2
¼	6	0.6	10	25.4	31	78.7
½	13	1.3	12	30.5	33	83.8
⅝	16	1.6	13	33.0	34	86.4
¾	19	1.9	14	35.6	35	88.9
⅞	22	2.2	15	38.1	36	91.4
1	25	2.5	16	40.6	37	94.0
1¼	32	3.2	17	43.2	38	96.5
1½	38	3.8	18	45.7	39	99.1
1¾	44	4.4	19	48.3	40	101.6
2	51	5.1	20	50.8	41	104.1
2½	64	6.4	21	53.3	42	106.7
3	76	7.6	22	55.9	43	109.2
3½	89	8.9	23	58.4	44	111.8
4	102	10.2	24	61.0	45	114.3
4½	114	11.4	25	63.5	46	116.8
5	127	12.7	26	66.0	47	119.4
6	152	15.2	27	68.6	48	121.9
7	178	17.8	28	71.1	49	124.5
8	203	20.3	29	73.7	50	127.0

yards to meters

yards	meters	yards	meters	yards	meters	yards	meters
⅛	0.11	2⅛	1.94	4⅛	3.77	6⅛	5.60
⅛	0.11	2⅛	1.94	4⅛	3.77	6⅛	5.60
¼	0.23	2¼	2.06	4¼	3.89	6¼	5.72
⅜	0.34	2⅜	2.17	4⅜	4.00	6⅜	5.83
⅝	0.46	2½	2.29	4½	4.11	6½	5.94
⅝	0.57	2⅝	2.40	4⅝	4.23	6⅝	6.06
¾	0.69	2¾	2.51	4¾	4.34	6¾	6.17
⅞	0.80	2⅞	2.63	4⅞	4.46	6⅞	6.29
1	0.91	3	2.74	5	4.57	7	6.40
1¼	1.03	3¼	2.86	5⅛	4.69	7¼	6.52
1¼	1.14	3¼	2.97	5¼	4.80	7¼	6.63
1⅜	1.26	3⅜	3.09	5⅜	4.91	7⅜	6.74
1½	1.37	3½	3.20	5½	5.03	7½	6.86
1⅝	1.49	3⅝	3.31	5⅝	5.14	7⅝	6.97
1¾	1.60	3¾	3.43	5¾	5.26	7¾	7.09
1⅞	1.71	3⅞	3.54	5⅞	5.37	7⅞	7.20
2	1.83	4	3.66	6	5.49	8	7.32

Index